Sandeep Parmar

Faust

Shearsman Books

First published in the United Kingdom in 2022 by
Shearsman Books
P O Box 4239
Swindon
SN3 9FN

Shearsman Books Ltd Registered Office
30–31 St. James Place, Mangotsfield, Bristol BS16 9JB
(this address not for correspondence)

www.shearsman.com

ISBN 978-1-84861-827-5

Faust

Contents

For my daughter, Gaia

I

FAUST

But see how, rising from this turbulence,
the rainbow forms its changing-unchanged arch,
now clearly drawn, now evanescent,
and casts cool, fragrant showers all about it.
Of human striving it's a perfect symbol—
ponder this well to understand more clearly
that what we have as life is many-hued reflection.
   —Goethe, *Faust*, Part II, Act I, 4715–4727, trans. Stuart Atkins

Yes, he can say to himself: Here on the most ancient, the eternal altar, built directly on the foundations of the world, I bring a sacrifice to the being of all beings.
   —Goethe, 'On Granite', trans. Norman Guterman

…that queer amalgamation of dream and reality, that perpetual marriage of granite and rainbow.
   —Virginia Woolf, 'The New Biography'

i.

I'd be but a shadow   seed of clay
    turned earth   blown onto the path of shadow

    Want or indigence   Debt or shame
        sisters of Distress   whose midnight phone calls
            light the bedside lamps
                you take the coverlet with you
  to the next room, Care, sister of Death
        where grief is not an abstraction but an inheritance   a waiting for

another dawn   a being   with sisters

        sageless arrows of grief

    we rain down our fury

        the devil whistles while he works

ii.

I am the fifth sister
        whose striving lays an ocean
                between the shadows of our dead

                quarrelling shores
                        a great distance apart

                here is your image
        a swan unfolding its wings
                a river of blood down its back
                        its beak preening at arterial speed
                                red feathers   foaming   unstopping flow

        we cross a mudded field of apple trees   in its dwindling harvest
                a circle of blonde heads   murmurous clutching arms
                        crouched webwork of ground

what magic is this   a conspiracy of daughters casting in daylight
        red and white   making sacrifice   of abject girlhood
                how have we come
                        to be here   sister

        the Autumn banks   the exile   of a grasslaid river

iii.

If I drew a line   through all our births   over five centuries
    from the Silk Road to the Sutlej
        through the woolly Khyber   its dark resin
            wending towards Lahore
                pockets of carved stones
        at one end would be the seed   ferrous imbricate hybrid
            yellowing thorn of wheat

At the other   distance   the June waking the July waking
    to inedible sheaves   to age
to our hair falling out, our eyes clouding with disease
    and the children   that keep on never coming

Father wild logic scythe in hand
barefoot harvesting all night
high on opium

iv.

You ride the elevator to the eleventh floor of a hotel
        the tallest in our seaside town
            pale yellow or coral or white
                no lighthouse but an abrasive plinth
                    chartered to the shore by cement.

Holy fathers, beatified men   their bronze or wooden statues dot the coast
        from San Diego to San Francisco
Up El Camino Real—
        where curved poles topped by soundless bells
                hang like sickles.

A river, a mission, a chapel, its garden.
        An ocean, a boardwalk, mountains, a freeway.
The town's Franciscan priest,
        Junípero Serra, once had his hands
doused with red paint. Genocidal
        churches, arable lands. A museum
with pieces of or whole Chumash
        bowls and other poorly-handled things.
School children appraise them. It is an annual ritual.

                    *

You request a room overlooking the Pacific.
The elevator does not stop; the hotel is never full.

A wooden pier—once of remarkable length—
        extends towards the Channel Islands,
draped in fog, reachable by boat

if you wake with the fishermen before dawn.
A novel was set in those islands about the sole
    inhabitant of San Nicolas. The facts are:
a native woman alone for eighteen years
    spotted on the beach skinning a seal;
hauled ashore to the mission where dysentery
    killed her and her language off. She was given
a Christian name. We read it in school
    but remember nothing except
the word Aleutian and a numbness
    sharpened by no response. It was written
by a descendent of Sir Walter Scott.
    Scott was, among other things, an early translator
of Goethe. Dear sister. What you have learned is a dying craft.

The elevator opens onto a quiver of directions.

*

You drift back to a rose garden, a small women's college
    where each girl is permitted to pick and take
all the roses she can carry back to her room.

*

The pier, battered by storms, is rebuilt. A catafalque
    decked in American flags from sternum to navel.
From this angle, the sea is a parade of elbow length satin.
    Excavating the cave of the lone woman at San Nicolas,
diggers were halted by the Navy. It lies half-dug,
    disputed, full of sand, making distress calls.
You run towards the end of the pier with your arms
    open, lodging in its sights like a gale or target.

*

The room's ceiling is shot white powder,
    liable to yellow and stain.
Someone later recalled seeing you taking
    in the view from your balcony.
The sun is flattening into the sea and below
    there are families fishing or striding
in the dimming orange light. It is well-beyond
    happy hour in the tiki-themed bar,
the seafood restaurant we thought was so sophisticated.
    There's a revolving ballroom,
long since closed, where high schools held their proms.
    Corsages, rented limos, hairspray,
saliva drying on gums in windy sunroofs. The sun
    is a gold disc over the grey-blue waters of the Pacific.

*

To strive, you think, to know. You've brought with you a copy of *Faust*. What is it to want to know everything. The light sharpens to a point to a full stop to an ingot of gold at 7.30 p.m. This alchemy. Do you open *Faust*. Do you leave it in the dingy room, on the beige bedspread, a wager of its own in our Eden this Arcadia. Faust's strip of coastline, a paradise built in his dotage, unbegun but in his imagination, an inner light. Now you remember everything. You are in a state of sudden alertness. You find your aim you strive. There is the sun, blinding all the summer day. There is the cliff, where Euphorion dropped into blackness marching heroic. You think of the roses and how you carried them all in your arms. Striding full of hope into another century. To want, to owe, to feel shame. Dear sister. To wish to know everything Faust says you must become nothing Mephistopheles says to extend beyond what is human you must become the Spirit of Eternal Negation Faust says you must be willing to die but I am not afraid to die Mephistopheles says I will route your indentured soul from an eye an ear a navel a fingernail for the jaws of hell are always open Faust love has waded through my many dreams and orchestrations Mephistopheles opines we were all girls in another century baring our arms in an inhabited garden Care slips through the keyhole like smoke a kind of being without a kind of alchemy Faust you will never fall where love can be seen from a great height rising above these hills like a memorable star.

v.

Go home then—

Why did you come here

To study (you tell the officer)

To retrace my steps part way home

Across a burning field

To stand in the smoke and to locate its source

To conquer this country back

To watch the black dog circle with its tail of fire

   The snares of our future bondage

To stand between a grandfather and his meat cleaver

Across a burning street

Where men carve flames into a glass shopfront and debouch into

Another burning street

A memory you steal or borrow

Heavy in my hand like a defunct currency

   A language

   To learn

vi.

Kernels of rain   or *seeds* of rain
     is how raindrops translate

so that even the rain is not itself
                                        when you wait mouth open
                                        looking sceptical or just pulling
                                        at the dry earth with broken lips.

Who will plant the rain   in a hearse so that the moon blooms
                                                            from his heart?
Grandfather, laid out and burnt like a stoic length of chaff,
his mind a prophecy of smoke.
     Two rupees in his breast pocket and a slip of white, neatly folded,
          with his son's address on it.

Smoke that is not rain nor wheat but leans
into them both like a fever
unmatched by the living.

There   he says, in a blue of white,
that is all you ever needed to know about wheat.

vii.

The wheat came apart in her hands

her hands came apart in the grass

her body a field

the field her body

innumerable hands would bury

Carry the charge

the imprisoned lightning
of her name

viii.

A landscape that repels description   this counterfeit Eden
    whose surfeit demands   you catalogue

but did not think to note its variety   merely its similitude
    of bougainvillea, agave, eucalyptus, orange wildflower

A cartilage of succulents, yellow synovials of kelp popping under
                                  your feet
        where nothing ages or dies

First I waited with a shovel   then I threw the shovel and ran

Lilac Creek overflowing
Romero   San Ysidro
    cottages roll into the sea over a cliff

  A child chokes on a deluge of mud
    slides into a living room
        on a wave
        under a coffee table
        his mouth a breach of tides
        someone gently empties

the sand and clay from his fists
A woman and her clever dog float to the surf

ix.

Who will we become
across several oceans—Arabian to Pacific—

rude stars
in an arc bending over Kyiv, Belarus, Astrakhan.

This ear that recognises its name and the words for water, hunger
learns

the cold sum   the clean sum.

You say   where there is water.
And the obvious truth of god.

A long long homecoming
across a field of ash
grain spilling a trail
from an unsealed urn.

x.

by soft coincidence
        by a chance crossing
of wild river grasses
        by seizing threshing seeding
by training the eye on green
        green wild soft unfolding
the seasonal miracle named
        by its naked composition
its durability also female
        by sowing and harvesting
incidentally woman given shape
        by burning off its chaff
by haploid shedding its goat
        face stricken by no word
for spring only weather
        coincidence of chance
the periodic flight
        from the sun's long shadow
by a known path
        which is why you take
your elders with you
        or else lose your way

xi.

Who will tear at their faces   for the Levantine or Persian
        extraction   the lost wheat   hold vigil at the pyre
        for whatever remains at dawn

To return home is to choke on the bread
        risen   that is no longer made

        this desi kanak like ash
        that carries your diurnal
        blood in its whiteness

You cling to it   or you don't   falling out of use

Someone else bows   touches fire to the feet
        of your dead

Gone
        the seed holds
                lodged in its thin neck
                        head swaying   driven out to

where your ancestors
were cut down   empty handed   crossing a border without shoes
where one day   you will sit   on dry earth with them

and eat your own flesh
shaking with pity

xii.

botanist	grass
chemist	organic compounds
geneticist	a challenging organism
farmer	a cash crop
hauler	freight
laborer	employment
merchant	produce
miller	grist
baker	flour
banker	chattel
politician	a problem
animals	feed
parasites	sustenance
conservationist	ground cover
religion	a symbol
artist	a model
a livelihood	lifegiving food

(cf. *Wheat and Wheat Improvement*, Karl Spangler Quisenberry, 1967)

In the book of dowries
everyone in its handwrit
ledger is in debt to each
other which is why
marriage must continue
so neighbours mither
sit crosslegged over
generational accounts
of poor past harvests
and dream of burning
the heavy handling

of ancestral losses
like a stubble of reeds
along with the thin man
whose family is charged
with preserving them
in carefully inked rows
but when otherwise
would the village gather
to listen to the given
names of their forefathers

Sonora, Lerma Roja,
their descendants took indigenous names
so each could be traced like male heirs
to caste family faith district acre season

Kaliyan meaning   the solution

A seed is not a jewel   a prized son   a golden interloper
to set in a collet
deposing all others

The grain as hands her hands as grain
The grain as light   dust as grain
As light as dust   her hands as seed
Grain as weather as moving through
The earth where grain falls she falls
Here as water sweetened after a fast
The grain she saw growing not as grain
Is your father in the marketplace
Grain cursed penniless, auctioned
Shuffling home unseasonable yields
Indelible shame and hunger its own
shame sets fire to grain plots a loss
standing over a jute sack of seed
that is his body and they appraise it
between fingers for the going rate
father if I could have bought a year
of wheat exchanged for bread you'd
stride powerfully as a boy as grain
in the hands of a mother regained
from the earth where she fell into
Bitter yellow rattle light this chance
      harvest

xiv.

The plough carves fate into flames that split your skull forty-six years after your birth. The *douleur,* the *gham,* the *tragedy* of six harvests overseen as the tumours weave like fire in your gut and the seventh, final crop you will never see breathes gently under the frost of Punjab. Shadows step inside you, capacious as a groom apprised of all he's won. Debt sown into the skin like disease, like one who, mad from silent protest, hapless, runs and runs into a headwind of bullets.

This is how it takes root, brother. You were too busy to notice. The bottle of Johnnie Walker exsanguinating between your palms like the prophet who squeezed blood from a rich man's bread into the sand refusing his table for the peasant's humble spread. *These potatoes, these onions, I have planted and dug for centuries and you bring me—an Englishman?* Sisters, stones in the soil at the best of times, crown your threshold carelessly on the day you die.

xv.

How is your family life? [my uncle]
You are living a half life. [my drycleaner]
You are living a stupid life. A stupid life. [a poet]

xvi.

The Traveller returns to the cottage on a hill of Philemon and Baucis, old childless couple. Years prior, they rescued him and his ship of goods strewn on the rocks, his eyes half-dead. Baucis wound her shawl across his chest and dragged him lifeless to the tall linden trees circling a chapel. Or was it Philemon who bellowed with his last drop of youthful vigour at the man to stand, palms open, making the Traveller stumble like an unborn son through sand dunes. Perhaps their charge grew familiar as the hearth lit his profile, coming to, or on forming early words, an ocean stirring in his chest, they turned away unsettled and blinked and bit their lips. *I have returned*, he said, seeing them so aged and the shore transplanted from their door to a distant port by technology. Chance or misfortune will not bring you twice to your destiny. This time the Traveller strove to throw himself into their arms, trudging up the leeward slope across forest and marsh. To strive to make his way home. *You will remember me from long ago.* Baucis prepares a meal and Philemon pours a shortage of wine. *Whom do you love?* How often the Traveller thought of being so saved. The fire's embers whirl into the sky. The smoke churns the far off covetous and lonely. Together, they pray. The chapel bell sways in a funerary dance. The devil and his strongmen stride up the narrow path. Silently, the three of them break their fast.

xvii.

On Walpurgisnacht   in the land of monsters   of half-women
    Lamiae cocottes admit the devil to their dance
    a murmuration of Sirens shift like a veil
    and other birds—goose-footed mouths of vultures—prophecy
    atop a primordial peak, flecked by fire

The Sphinx asks for your name
        an unsolvable riddle

You, questing spirit
    hewn from granite
        you war-storied obelisk
        you unripe grain of corn
        you daughter of abominations
        you sister of Mephistopheles
        you Faust lusting for Helen
        you who cannot stand your ground
        you who mount—and then cling to—a horse that never stops

xviii.

You held the long-forgotten cup to your lips
    a sharp reasoning   to lessen your striving

Old magician, doctor, survivor of plague,
    hypocrite scholar   whose strangulation cure

Gave fame to his mercy. Knowledge-maker, spirit
    of the Earth, of the sky   inscriber of pentagrams

Inviting in he who rings the bell   for Christ is risen
    knocking the wine from your hand   whose poison

packs your suitcase, waves goodbye to your kin, burns
    every house   eternally   within arm's reach

xix.

We see the flatterer   coming up the path   through a single eye
   We sisters, monsters grey from birth, keeping counsel in our cave
      We graceless Graeae, kin to Gorgons, Fates, we Phorcides
         who pass between us one eye, one sharp tooth
            We who cannot see the devil all at once
               But know his many guises

He, the procurer of certificates.
He, the forger of passports.
He, who is paid only in cash.
He, a forgetter of faces.
He, a registrar, a bursar, bank manager,
         a purser, a pilot, border patrol officer,
         a suitor, a celebrant, senior doctor.

Scatter yourselves
over the earth,
he ordered.
Go at once
you seedless
women;
you beasts.

So I have taken the eye, and left you our shared tooth.

What I have seen, dear sister.

   If you can name yourself, no riddle will remain

xx.

Faust: *There is no past or future in an hour like this, the present*

                                      moment only

Helen: *is our bliss*   [Goethe]

Child, whose name is abundance
  who leans into a drift rising
    heroic into a war
      across a wingless ocean   this rumour this child
        whose very happiness depends on battle
        whose body will disappear into the body
          of a man and then into the unholy
          darkness that unknowable shore
          of the ground descending
          alone or into the wide sky
          as mist the body whose leaving
          is untouched gleaming untarnished
          whose parents lean into a present becoming
          quickly past whose name means everywhere
          a loss I catalogue each moment its noble fall
          holding fast—mother—to these clothes that scorch
          and draw up like smoke clouds this body is the last child
          these clothes sewn by my hands you have long since
                                 outgrown

xxi.

I mulched the roses for your physic,
the Doctor says, lopping each head
into a good sterile jar. Tomorrow
I will sow these fermented blooms
back into your lungs, its opal tincture
an apotheosis of rainwater injected
into the body on trial. The townsfolk,
drawn by some popular ritual or by an
unharvested crop will macerate spring
bulbs back into the earth, ploughing
on a saint's day, dancing in a beerish
circle, claiming I am their protector.
—I confess to you what salves are poisons
what passes for heroism, I weep, I laugh
loudly, knowing only the devil knows—
that sharp-elbowed CEO at the lectern
scalding the lawn brown like herbicide.
I signed a contract in my blood to strive.
A reporter starts up, corrects himself,
gets my name right, right again, wrong.

xxii.

That we cannot recall a single dinner conversation
That we always ate cross-legged on newspaper
That we (sometimes) had a dining room table
That our tables were (sometimes) cardboard boxes
That boxes were half of everything we owned
That none of our dinner tables would survive
That no conversation prepared you for my leaving
That we were so unprepared for what we endured

xxxiii.

Even the wives and children of the prophets are not spared the return of fire

—it is late I cannot show you where I have thrown the good seed

Who would trust the white devil to fetch a pail of water to break his crown

—it is late you cannot harvest what has taken root among the thorns

Even the mothers of mothers walked through flames to spare his namesake

—who lit the weeds and wheat refusing the bargain it is too late to know

     a *knowledgeable unknowing*   a girl breaking loose running

xxiv.

the language of the saints (Gurmukhi)

the language of the king (Shahmukhi)

cross this burning line

hot sticky mustard seed

a late winter crop

whose meaning

clings inseparably

to the melting skins

of my devoted

xxv.

He that hath ears, let him hear. [Matthew 13:9]

In a palmed square, staged for an ancient drama
you appear as Old Iniquity, a man of shrunken
goat-hoof in a riddle of circadian spheres. Pour
the fino—flowering a fist that turns bread to wine
wine to bread—vain general trained at rhetoric
by ancestral magnates in provincial misericords.
In the tall shadow of the archaeological museum
you are every busted remnant of war under glass
that once pertained to great civilisations. Come
fire, its purge, with you at the bellows. Turn blood
to vapour. I am certain that with your cold blue
eye you sized up our village, its grasses lodging.
You weighed the iron and sold us back its alloy
cheap, melting down family names etched there
for dowries. An object is only worth its use—
and what use is memory. You, whose forgetting
pawns itself in grief. I remember how at the wall
you pissed an apology over ruined stones, a white
road leading you back to England. Drawing a line
that we must cross and cross again towards you,
old enemy, dragging dark symbols into the sun.

xxvi.

Warning, in music-words / devout and large, /
that we are each other's / harvest
                              —Gwendolyn Brooks

Wretched girl, there you go
        flashing in beads of glass, a silver-

laid comb, a mirror, gifts of the devil
        from your disguised suitor, who

wanting nothing but to break your striving
        in faith, in love, in youth

would make your family crawl
        on his orders or be flogged—*O*

you think I am a beast? I will marry you
        and your daughters and make

them crawl and their daughters having
        disbanded their sons will crawl

on their bellies like the worm and gather
        your hair like sheaves every April

a mystery rite, a crime scene, cupped palms
        burning with an inedible seed.

                    *

Psyche made my work easy, so did Helen,
but you are a girl so simple that destroying
you loses my interest. Throw yourself
from a cliff, the ramparts, where no wind
will save or split your body from its skin.

*

She, honestly risen on the singing ash of her
neighbours, makes a poor offering to Faust.
Her first death was beauty, her second that
he should replace her god, her third by her
own hand. O, to be an ecstatic field of grass.

*

I married the devil but he brought me back.
Shadow woman wearing a collar of knives.
Separable from all that is mine or was hers.
Every circle cries like a starved, angry child.
Even my slippers with their red velvet eyes.

*

The tributaries of the Indus—fingers across
a throat or arm of a girl bolting through
grasses. *Landrace* is that the word for her
slow dying. A box of scent from the queen
of the underworld. O, mothers, wash me.

xxvii.

Your heart packs up its mismatched syntax

In another room your husband

Is typing typing

The ladies in Barbour jackets are so nice

They sing to themselves on their morning walks

Go back to sleep he says

Streetlights go off one after another

It is some ritual

Come to pieces

Like a mausoleum

For a first wife

At the altar a third figure

Burned who you also married

He is in another room

Sterilising the linens in a churn

Singing his goatfoot steaming

Go back to sleep he says

I re-read the book of myths

The ash falling from my hair onto its pages

—*You were young and beautiful once, too, ho ho hee hee*

xxviii.

'…civilization is a process in the service of Eros, whose purpose is to combine single human individuals, and after that families, then races, peoples and nations, into one great unity, the unity of mankind.'

[Freud, *Civilization and its Discontents*]

You're pathetic, a joke—

See this line

     You can't see

Crawl over it

     On your belly

Like the snake   a degenerate race

     You will know by my tone

When you've crossed it

     this mudded field   a holy shrine

     turned over   the Devil knows

I do God's work   keeping you in line

It   it is   this shape

     A shadow

Your very best side   your very last words

     Tightening around your throat

xxviv.

Faust: What happens now?
Mephistopheles: Direct your strivings downward.

Follow the river, sisters. Follow the beasts
who walk the threshing circle, doomed, blind
beside the man who put out their eyes. Follow
the mist-sacred ground, the *bad coin of fear*
inverted, to the last home we would ever know.

II

A Winnowing Shovel

In 2002, the Spanish cultural psychiatrist Joseba Achotegui developed the term *Ulysses Syndrome* to describe a set of stress-induced disorders seen in migrants suffering harsh living conditions in their adopted homelands. In otherwise mentally healthy individuals, Achotegui noted the prevalence of symptoms such as migraines, insomnia, recurrent worrying, nervousness, irritability, disorientation, fear, and gastric and osteo-physical pains, symptoms that aren't uniquely experienced by migrants but are linked to complex migration: to the struggle to survive, to belong, to a sense of failure, to social isolation and cultural loss, to acculturation in a hostile host nation. He calls it a picture of 'extreme migratory grief' and, citing Odysseus's reply to the cyclops Polyphemus (that he is no man), suggests that if you must become nobody to survive you become permanently invisible. But to be a hero may be the precise opposite of this, and I am reminded of the classicist Jane Ellen Harrison's *Ancient Art and Ritual* (1913) which draws a bridge between the communal, spiritual desire in ancient ritual to the impulse towards the creation of art—both differently serve the emotional needs of their society at critical moments through enactment and representation. Harrison compares them thus, writing that 'In the old ritual dance the individual was nothing, the choral band, the group, everything, and in this it did but reflect primitive tribal life. Now in the heroic saga the individual is everything, the mass of the people, the tribe, or the group, are but a shadowy background which throws up the brilliant, clear-cut personality into a more vivid light.' Harrison's primary interest in ritual is at odds with the heroic impulse, for it is in the shared ritual that we come to understand human society and its fears and hopes, not in its exemplars, those heroes bathed in light and literary glory. For her there is no such thing as a heroic society. In her synthesising both ancient and modern worlds, Harrison writes 'in a word, the heroic spirit, as seen in heroic poetry, is the outcome of a society cut loose from its roots, of a time of migrations, of the shifting of populations.' The wandering hero, whose glorious deeds guarantee his fame, is of course nowhere in evidence in the mass migrations of the twentieth and twenty-first centuries nor in its literary representations. Such involuntary migrations tethered to world wars, empire, genocide, climate crisis, globalisation, economic drivers, etc, if made heroic or exceptional commit a kind of violence on its subject. And yet conversely, the body of the migrant is perceived as plural, invasive; this multiplicity is a dehumanisation built into the very language we use to speak about migration. To be a hero in the modern sense is to be someone who anyone could be and is therefore, also, no one.

But what of the case of voluntary migration? The self that makes itself heroic by remaking, in striving away from home, striving for gain, whose journey is chosen but whose stresses and grief are in some ways not dissimilar to Achotegui's figuration of complex migration? How is striving itself, as an idea built into literary models and real-life stereotypes of the good immigrant or the model minority, how might striving—in the Faustian sense—provide a way of thinking about heroism, tragedy (modern and ancient) and migratory grief? Who chooses to leave and why, who attempts to return, who stays on, who, to borrow from Bhanu Kapil's image of reverse migration, is made psychotic in a national space, who is this hero who journeys, who strives and for what? To be visible or invisible? As others have looked to the Faust legend for ways to explore the insatiability of man's appetites, the questions I put to Goethe's version specifically bring together three strands: striving as a fear of and countermeasure against mortality; a critique of globalisation and technology; and the female element counteracting male aggression, destruction and desire.

For me, these questions emerge from a personal, ancestral misery. On both sides of my family—who are linked closely by tribal bonds, a caste-bound brotherhood of intermarriages going back centuries—we have moved further and further from home for as far back as can be traced. In the early part of the nineteenth century, my ancestors had a flexible existence—they made their home on the banks of the Chenab river in what is now Pakistan; they farmed a little, largely for their own use, they made their living twisting reeds into rope and baskets. It wasn't until, as I understand it, the British apportioned forest land to those who would commit to clearing and cultivating it in the mid-19th century that my family became bound to agriculture. A network of canals was built in Punjab, the land of the five rivers, what would become the breadbasket of a newly-independent India. Drawing from a somewhat romantic, orientalist viewpoint, Marx critiqued what he saw as the colonial degradation of rural village life by colonial systems of governance and bureaucracy as the onset of capitalism, of farming driven by profit rather than the benefit of the community. A denaturing of the old ways, Marx foresaw, would lead to famines. In the *New York Daily Tribune* in 1853, Marx decries the 'spectacle of the crumbling of an ancient world', a sort of nostalgia for a world order that had already crumbled in the West. He ends somewhat ambivalently by quoting from Goethe's capacious, orientalising poetic dialogue between east and west, the *Diwan*: "Should this torture then torment us / Since it brings us greater pleasure? / Were not through the rule of Timur / Souls devoured without measure?"

What is gained when one home is lost, and another is offered in its place as you walk and as you are driven over the earth in such torment? The British would relinquish the cultivation of their land, to be farmed and taxed and nominally owned, until their withdrawal in 1947. Partition, for those who managed to stake a claim in an imaginary new nation for an equivalent land holding, meant exchanging your farm for another farm of equal size over an imaginary line. If you could reach it. Here the story accelerates: industrial farming on the scale promised by the Green Revolution of the 1960s led to bigger harvests, more technology, expensive machinery, irrigation canal and dam building, pesticides, fertilisers. Nothing could be further a hundred years later from life on the banks of the Chenab. This is how I understand it. That in the edible grasses growing under your feet you might remember the harvest you never made on the land from which you fled. That you arrive to harvest someone else's abandoned season and find that on leaving they destroyed all of their wells. That one year's harvest—some five thousand rupees—might buy a plane ticket for a son to go to England and to eventually send money home—that if he failed, you ate seed borrowed on credit for as long as you could to survive. That you make heroes of your children because someone set fire to your house across an invisible border and you can't stop running. So you start striving. A better house, a better job, more money. You disband, are disbanded. The shadowy background of the choral band recedes like ghosts in the underworld.

To return to Ulysses: in Homer's Book XI, Odysseus recounts meeting his mother in hell. He hasn't gone looking for her; he didn't know she was dead. He digs a pit; he sacrifices two sheep; their blood runs into the trench; the hero holds the assembling ghosts at bay who are drawn to drink from it with his sword. Asking how she died, his mother replies 'my longing to know what you were doing and the force of my affection for you—this it was that was the death of me' [tr. Butler]. Odysseus repeatedly attempts to embrace his mother and each time she dematerialises, a phantom form, unreachable. It is the blind prophet Tiresias who Odysseus seeks, and he instructs him how best to make the passage safely back to his kingdom; but follows this up with a further labour: to make peace with Poseidon who he has angered and who torments his return home after a twenty years' absence.

> But once you have killed those suitors in your halls—
> by stealth or in open fight with slashing bronze—
> go forth once more, you must...
> carry your well-planed oar until you come
> to a race of people who know nothing of the sea,
> whose food is never seasoned with salt, strangers all
> to ships with their crimson prows and long slim oars,
> wings that make ships fly. And here is your sign—
> unmistakable, clear, so clear you cannot miss it:
> When another traveller falls in with you and calls
> that weight across your shoulder a fan to winnow grain,
> then plant your bladed, balanced oar in the earth
> and sacrifice fine beasts to the lord god of the sea,
> Poseidon—a ram, a bull and a ramping wild boar—
> then journey home and render noble offerings up
> to the deathless gods who rule the vaulting skies,
> to all the gods in order.
> [tr. Fagles, XI, 136–152]

This final task feels unnecessary, even unfair. An added labour onto the hero's journey now ended that extends the narrative's natural resolution of return, conquest, the restoration of the king. The work of return is never done. And perhaps this is the migrant's striving: to make home where home can never be made, to carry what is familiar into a place of unfamiliarity and to repurpose it in a place of unbelonging, a place where you risk being no one. Perhaps this is the migrant's grief-sodden task, sent on an errand to sate forces greater than themselves, to never tarry, to distrust happiness, beset by longing. My mother's first memory is of a grain harvest in Punjab, of a winnowing shovel throwing freshly threshed wheat into the air and the hot chaff sticking to her face. I have never seen a wheat harvest up close—the combines that roam the fields in August around where I live in semi-rural Lancashire are decidedly joyless. The pain of false recognition builds a temple in its own image to satisfy what angry god. Yet we continue to build.

*

On the night of August 15th 1947 my grandfather climbed to the roof of his house. From where he stood he could see his city burning. To one side were the fields he owned in the dark distance. And the sound of unhoming, forcibly or voluntarily taking whatever you could carry or tie onto a cart. But he felt no urgency to leave. Anyway, what is fire. It will extinguish itself by morning, he might have thought. No one alive remembers his house. What were his children doing and his second wife, the first taken by death in her childbearing years? His eldest son urged them to run, to fight, to stand their ground. What is fire anyway for the young. What is it for your elders.

On a night in December 2017, my father spotted a fire spilling down the hillside in Ventura, California. An alchemical line to a scientist is oxygen, fuel, toxic fumes in parts per million, wind speed and probabilities—proximities to death. He and my mother lay in bed watching it, wondering whether to sleep. What is fire but a chain of reactions waiting to exhaust itself. We should go, he said. My mother, unpicking passports and photographs from what might reasonably be left to burn, refused. We should stay and fight, she insisted. What is fire to a mother who has walked through death for each of her children. She knows the weight and composition of the house, how combustible every corner is and could arm herself with a shovel and tie back her hair. Fire is also her own mother crossing a newly-drawn border through fire and leaving everything in her home behind to burn.

On the night of [redacted] my childhood friend's elder sister [redacted] rented a hotel room in our hometown with a balcony overlooking the Pacific. From where she stood she could have seen as far as the Channel Islands to the west, to the east in the hillsides were both our houses. Her house yet unconsumed by the fires of 2017 that were captured by a security camera mounted on an eave. She took nothing with her but a copy of Goethe's *Faust*. From there, around sunset, she jumped. I remember her and her love of the German language. That in the '90s, she was a goth. I remember her great kindness and how elder sisters are like gods. How her family had fled the Holocaust. How much I have wondered about her love of the German language.

What is home but a waiting for, a fire to which we must return. The myth of another century bearing down on the horizon like a galleon. Once you leave home you can never be at home anywhere; someone will always be quick to point to a road or a mountain assuming you hadn't already spilled blood there so know it intimately. Something set us going that won't let go.

*

In Marshall Berman's reading of *Faust* as exemplary of the modern condition, he posits that Faust's development of self is tied to economic development, that Faust's story is indeed the *tragedy of development*. In one way, we see this most clearly in Faust's ambitious final project—a canal system that fights the force of the ocean to reclaim a coastal strip of land. Faust, who begins as the scholar in Goethe's part one, ends as an imperial figure appropriating land for an imagined project of development as both philanthropy and avarice. Having made a wager over his soul to never tarry, to never stop and enjoy the beauty of the moment, to ceaselessly strive, Faust loses... but this is not the tragedy of Goethe's subtitle. It is not in the classical sense that *Faust* is tragic for the modern and hence more reflective post-Enlightenment Man doesn't suffer in the pattern set forth by myth or divine design; he suffers his own choices with full knowledge of their consequences (Kierkegaard). Faust's self-development is also a series of tragic failures to grasp the moral and at times social dimensions of his own wish for omnipotence.

As Freud would lean on Goethe's *Faust* to develop his ideas of the Death Instinct, of Mephistopheles as aggressor and antithesis of creation (he calls himself the spirit of negation) and finally in *Civilisation and its Discontents* to link narcissism with the Nazis, we see the individual's wish for omnipotence (a kind of heroism) as the enemy of mankind. On the female presence in *Faust* there is much, really too much to say. But three groups of women interest me most: the Mothers, a shadowy group of ancients who provide Faust the means to retrieve Helen of Troy from the afterlife is the first, the second are simply referred to as Four Women ghosts, sisters who precipitate Faust's downfall: they are personifications of Want, Debt, Distress and Care. Faust is in the process of completing his land development project and has just had the elderly couple Philemon and Baucis, whose house stands in his way of total conquest, killed by Mephistopheles and his henchmen. The conversation between Faust and Care results in her blinding him, having promised him unending torment and dissatisfaction with any achievement. One might well argue that Faust throughout the play is already driven by this constant anxiety and dissatisfaction, this 'companion-cause of fear' by striving for material gain in the present moment. But what changes is Faust's will for a legacy, a hoped for afterlife through his deeds on earth, fame and remembrance. And this thought triggers the end of his wager. Ultimately Faust is saved from damnation by god's grace and female intervention—the wronged Gretchen from *Faust* Part 1 and Christian female figures of the divine, the third group of women significant to Faust's story. Whatever creative or erotic impulse Faust's earth-bound feats demonstrate—from seductions to diplomacy to marshland retrieval to the invention of paper money and the expansion of empires—the play ends with the chorus proclaiming 'Woman, eternally, shows us the way'. They are the not just the physically beautiful but idealised forms on which truth relies, as Walter Pater's essay on Johann Joachim Winckelmann and Goethe naturally associates a marrying of the romantic with the Hellenic in the figures of the Mothers. The Mothers, even their mention, makes Faust shudder.

Faust parts 1 and 2 took Goethe sixty years to write from an early sketched-out version we know of now as the *Urfaust* to its final posthumously published version. The idea of *Faust* haunted him for almost his entire life—he first witnessed *Faust* as a puppet play in childhood, so common was the myth of the magician and necromancer—and we know that amid his other many works including scientific treatises on colour, plants, geology, *Faust* was always in his mind, always ready to spring into action as Goethe's world view and quest for understanding science and art became more and more insatiable. We see the imprint of this expansive learning—some of his theories proved to be foolish, others prescient—throughout his *Faust* in rainbows and granite—Woolfian binaries not far from Goethe's own imagining. Goethe's life bridges, it has often been said, many crucial rendings from the old to the new world of industrialisation, secularism, empire, and capitalism. We return continually to his version of *Faust*, second only in English to Marlowe's version and a distant cousin to Thomas Mann's dark reworking of the legend. Serendipity and a life of learning guide Goethe's play, the force of it pulls anything even remotely close to it into its orbit.

And, finally, another serendipity—serendipity as a mode of poetics is how I generally work and how this essay, too, is shaped. Among the many translators of Goethe's *Faust* was the Northern Irish poet Louis MacNeice who, along with a literal translator, adapted it for BBC Radio in 1949 to mark the bicentenary of his birth. MacNeice wrestled with the task not because he found it linguistically challenging but, as his notes to the Faber edition of his translation state, because so much of *Faust* is digressive, lengthy and unrelated to the central plot and characters. MacNeice set about trimming Goethe, drawing the listener's attention to Faust the man, his actions and desires. With an eye for a hero. I read his *Faust* with interest, note the staging of good and evil, of action rather than context. I turn to MacNeice, his life and homeland, his measured political stance as a poet and BBC features reporter for the Home Service. MacNeice in 1949 had not long returned from India, where he made a few documentary features about the end of the Raj and on Partition. His letters to his wife Hedli and indeed a poem called 'Letter from India' give us a sense of what he saw—mixing with intellectuals, political figures like Nehru and the poet Sarojini Naidu, Krishna Menon—and his anxiety at the coming violence. Poignantly, at the lavish final party given by Lord Mountbatten at Viceroy's House in Delhi, the band plays 'Old

Man River', a song about the pain of enslavement most famously sung by actor and anti-imperialist Paul Robeson. The silence of the river, its indifference to human suffering, is history's ambivalence to the individual.

The producer accompanying MacNeice in India, Vaughan Thomas, recalls the violence they saw as they crossed a dividing country:

> I remember once driving with Louis to a little village called Shakpura. We got there to find that there'd been a terrible massacre that very morning... and suddenly I saw a totally different Louis, one I never imagined existed. Louis the man of action. He ordered those people into a nearby lorry, we got some sort of structure going of a way to get them out of the refugee area into something like safety and suddenly he was ordering people about, they were obeying him—a totally different Louis I suddenly saw revealed and also a Louis that was no longer the detached observer but one deeply and profoundly involved in the human dilemma.

MacNeice writes about this moment in the aforementioned 'Letter from India':

> I have seen Sheikhupura High School
> Fester with glaze-eyed refugees
> And the bad coin of fear inverted
> Under Purana Kila's trees
> And like doomed oxen those and these
> Cooped by their past in a blind circle;
>
> And day by day, night upon nightmare,
> Have spied old faults and sores laid bare,
> Line upon lineless, measureless under
> Pretended measure, and no air
> To feed such premises as where
> A private plot would warrant shelter.

MacNeice never mentioned or wrote about his actions as Vaughan describes them and instead retains the position of detached observer in his poem. Did he carry this inward sense of horror at human suffering, violence, evil, imperial power, into his remaking of *Faust*? It is impossible to say. But I cannot read his version of *Faust* without this knowledge. And with that, too, I bring the personal story of my own family seeking refuge in tents on the grounds of a different high school during Partition, some miles away, bound to their migratory fate across three continents like their abandoned bullocks locked in a threshing circle. I imagine what these refugees, turned economic migrants would finally wager their souls for. Think of how progress, how striving, is so encoded into the life of the immigrant that we find ourselves turning into any usable, familiar object. How they might plant their oar. For whom they would build a temple.

Sources:

Joseba Achotegui, *Ulysses Syndrome: The Immigrant Syndrome of Chronic and Multiple Stress* (Ediciones el Mundo de la Mente, 2015)

Marshall Berman, *All that is Solid Melts Into Air: The Experience of Modernity* (New York, NY: Simon and Schuster, 1982)

Sigmund Freud, *Civilization and its Discontents*, trans. by James Strachey, ed. by Peter Gay (New York, NY: W. W. Norton & Company, 1989)

Johann Wolfgang von Goethe, *Faust Parts 1 & 2*, trans. by Louis MacNeice (London: Faber & Faber, 1951)

—— trans. by Stuart Atkins (Princeton, NJ: Princeton University Press, 2014)

Jane Ellen Harrison, *Ancient Art and Ritual* (London: Williams and Norgate, 1913)

Homer, *The Odyssey*, trans. by Robert Fagles (New York, NY: Viking Penguin; London: Penguin Books, 1996)

—— trans. by Samuel Butler (London: Longman, 1900)

John Henry Jones, ed., *The English Faust Book: A Critical Edition Based on the Text of 1592* (Cambridge: Cambridge University Press, 2011)

Bhanu Kapil, *Schizophrene* (New York, NY: Nightboat Books, 2011)

Louis MacNeice, *Collected Poems* (London: Faber & Faber, 2007)

Louis MacNeice, *Selected Letters of Louis MacNeice*, ed. by Jonathan Allison (London: Faber & Faber, 2010)

Rüdiger Safranski, *Goethe: Life as a Work of Art*, trans. by David Dollenmayer (New York, NY: Liveright, 2019)

John Stallworthy, *Louis MacNeice* (London, Faber & Faber, 2011)

An Uncommon Language

The doctor says it's an empty room in there

And it is

A pale sack with no visitors
I have made it and surrounded it with my skin
To invite the baby in

But he did not enter
And dissolved himself into the sea so many moons ago

   (Dorothea Lasky, 'The Miscarriage')

It is said that 1 in 4 women miscarry at some point in their lives. Yet why are there so few poems about miscarriage, something that many women evidently experience? Why is this private and unseen loss near invisible or taboo, to speak or write about? Dorothea Lasky's poem was a discovery for me. And it is stark, perfect, detached, even. Its refrain, 'Work harder!' speaks to the exhausting demands on women's lives and bodies from a (western capitalist) society bent on the forward momentum of (re)production. Likewise, Fiona Benson's lyrical poems about miscarriage from *Bright Travellers* reframe human loss via the natural world in 'Sheep' and 'Prayer'. Sharon Olds and Lucille Clifton boldly describe the visceral experience of miscarrying. From this memory, both poets retrieve the lost child and imagine them into a (racial, marital, personal) history, where they otherwise have no physical presence in lived time.

   you threw off your
   working clothes of arms and legs,
   and moved house, from uterus
   to toilet bowl and jointed stem

and sewer out to float the rivers and
bays in painless pieces.

(Olds, 'To Our Miscarried One, Age Thirty Now')

the time i dropped your almost body down
down to meet the waters under the city
and run one with the sewage to the sea
what did i know about waters rushing back
what did i know about drowning
or being drowned

(Clifton, 'the lost baby poem')

These are some examples among what I suspect is a minor note in the
canon of women's writing. There has been, of late increasingly so, what
seems like a flowering of poems and whole collections about mother-
hood. But how might poems about miscarriage, its silence, broaden our
picture of maternity, a range of experiences, too often co-opted by the
logic and language of productivity?

Sylvia Plath's poem reflecting on her own miscarriage, 'Parliament Hill
Fields', I already knew but had not read attentively. It is not the 'bald
hill' or 'faceless' sky where the lost child's 'doll grip lets go' that stopped
me on re-reading it this time, but the line: 'I suppose it's pointless to
think of you at all'. This teaches us something about grieving, perhaps,
and its point. Although I also recalled reading Plath's radio poem
drama, *Three Women*, at least fifteen or more years ago, I never listened
closely to the three voices in it. Perhaps I flipped past it, thought one
day I might return to this poem about maternity when its consequences
applied to me. Back then, I couldn't differentiate clearly between the
'happy' mother of a son; the 'reluctant' mother who gives her daughter
up; and, of course, the woman in between, the 'second voice', who
miscarries. Now, for me, the second voice is the most compelling.
She identifies as dying, dead, death. She has lost a 'dimension'. She is
pointless, flat, has created no new face. But other faces, the 'faceless faces
of important men', nations, society, governments, all conspire against

women who have the power to produce new living dimensions. Who are not otherwise pointless.

> I am not ugly. I am even beautiful.
> The mirror gives me back a woman without deformity.
> The nurses give me back my clothes, and an identity.
> It is usual, they say, for such a thing to happen.
> It is usual in my life, and the lives of others.
> I am one in five, something like that. I am not hopeless.
> I am beautiful as a statistic. Here is my lipstick.

But grief is not pointless, its mourning or melancholy offers something when there is nothing to show for death. Where is the special language of grief given to women who miscarry? Does the expression of this particular grief rely on a borrowed tongue, more so than any particular love, or especial happiness, grief's necessary antecedents? I look everywhere for a way to wrench it from the mouths of doctors and nurses. Stillbirths, yes, there are brave books. The deaths of children, too, who have taken breath. But so little I find beyond the 'author unknown' postings on websites—a pop up asks if I want a 'grief friend'—and the exchanges between women who carry a secret death that make friends and family flounder for *the right words*.

In Helen Charman's powerful essay, 'Parental Elegy', she explores Complicated Grief Syndrome in poetry via Denise Riley's *Time Lived, Without its Flow* and both Jahan Ramazani's and Andrea Brady's works on the elegy. Charman writes that 'The relationship between productivity, parenthood and mourning reinforces, rather than alleviates, the 'complicated' problem of grief and narrative.' What are the ethics of producing poetry from grief, if that grief is pointless, finds no point, speaks back to death with an illegitimately and imprecisely acquired language?

§

You are no philosopher. Every time you speak of this kind of death you fear you are exaggerating. Death is real; what happened to you is not this but some unspeakable loss. A fact that cannot be explained by the framework of life, its order. You have no language of your own only a remote vocabulary, borrowed from mourning mothers, hoarse as Demeters, each heroic—and you are not this fact at all.

When a woman with certain privileges is about to give birth there's a slog of learning. Guides in print and thousands of websites. Most of which do not entertain other outcomes. Gradually, you pick it up, the knack of counting your life in weeks. Consider buying one of the many new books on motherhood, mostly by middle-class white women. You learn what it means to [redacted]. You feel the energy quietly being sapped away from you and the plurality of an internal conversation. When you inform the midwife you're opting for a consultant-led birth, she's surprised that 'an intelligent woman like you would make that decision'. You throw her a forced smile. What must it be like to see you or some version of you over and over day after day. Making the wrong decisions. Not quite English. The NHS leaflets piled thick in your palm. The hostile posters on the wards threatening those without legal status. This woman of the State is disappointed in you. But, anyway, you never see her again. You stop talking to your selves.

The woman's body is adrift. You find sisters to nurse you. *Her body is a graveyard*, A says. M explains: *miscarriages haunt women down generations*. S, who suffered a stillbirth, messages: *this is a minor moment in a woman's life that, at the time, feels major*. B emails you a spell. D and V are both Americans; they advise on the right drugs and procedures. P, blood sister, doctor, keeps you talking: *don't go quiet on me*. Miscarriage is its own language—clinicians keep it alive whereas women listen to its cold music and then forget, or try to. What would it be to keep this language in common use. To claim it back. Did women ever share ways to explain this to each other and to themselves? 'Language cannot do everything', Adrienne Rich advises in her 'Cartographies of Silence'. The scream /of an illegitimate voice // It has ceased to hear itself, therefore / it asks itself // How do I exist?'

M notes that in India even men know what a *D&C* is. Why is that? Your family would never acknowledge the shame that is pregnancy.

Aunties moving heavy with sin that gave your sister and you nightmares for at least thirty years. Neither would they speak of female feticide or amniocentesis, an antenatal means by which one can determine sex. But you know your Aunties have heard this language misused against them. Those Uncles who bluntly ask their wives or mistresses to cut into their insides by the right name.

You say, to your husband, 'if all goes well'. You say *you* because it's not your body. You imagine time reeling forward.

And, when the future stops, all is not well. You say 'I', but not aloud— an unspent curse. What is language anyway. An agreement. To make reparations. With whom. For what.

§

A world gone quiet must be this fact.
For which there is no precise language.
The monitor goes off and you are led
past a succession of mothers to a room marked 'empty'.
Taxonomies of grief elude the non-mother,
the un-mothered, the anything-but-this-fact.
No face no teeth no eyes or balled up fists.
To light the dark with a particular breathing.
A black lamp beats its wings ashore.

In the dark there is breathing.
After five visits to the hospital, the bruising
of inner elbows stitching themselves to themselves
in obsolescence, the nurses stop saying: *sorry for your loss*.
I may come to miss these laminated hallways.
I know my way there, to the artefact of losing.

Loosened from the factual world into a silence
where there is no grave but your own self stumbling
from floor to ceiling without an inch of your life.
Or mine. Or this particular absence.

The Lancastrian nurse is matter of fact.
Her metaphors are agrarian; the language of slaughter.
If you start bleeding like a stuck pig.
Under those thick white fingers an ancestry
of collapsing valves and bleating
transfigure into notes. You look familiar.
Why have you come here, again,
to my door with your metaphors of slaughter.

A folder, yellow, the word *baby*
on its cover, re-filed as miscellaneous.
What grew in you is not you but a shroud
and any idiot knows a shroud.
A ghost who wakes you up five times a night
stands undecided between rooms
shivering in its thin shadow.
I know my way here, to the language of loss.

My grandmother, who died giving birth,
explains what makes carnelian so red.
I assumed it was the iron in its veins
that made the Romans stamp their profiles
onto its brittle clots. Pulse of empire.

Don't say that / I never visited you.
A ghost is as good a family / as you may get.
Va, itni der baad thusi aaye hai?
After all this time, you've finally come?
The child that clawed you towards death is my kin.
His bones are a line pressed into the earth

you never wanted to cross, transfigured on the back
of a convoy somewhere else. It must be this fact.

A village and its farms and its wells
On an ordinary day in August
smell of blood and panic
carrying a child from this and that
disease, whose death is on your hands.

You look familiar. Why have you come here.

Blighted or to *blight*. What gives up gives over
is absorbed back into itself like a harp gone quiet
imperceptibly in the night.

SOURCES:

Lucille Clifton, *How to Carry Water: Selected Poems* (Rochester, NY: BOA
        Editions, 1987)
Dorothea Lasky, *Milk* (Seattle, WA: Wave Books, 2018)
Sharon Olds, *Stag's Leap* (New York, NY: Knopf; London: Jonathan Cape,
        2012)
Sylvia Plath, *Three Women*, in *Winter Trees* (London: Faber & Faber, 1971);
        Collected Poems (London: Faber & Faber, 1981)

III

The Nineties

This is our fear of 'the other'
– Indians, blacks, Mexicans, Communists, Muslims, whatever –
America has to have its monsters,
so we can zone them, segregate them,
if possible, shoot them.
                    —Robin Robertson, *The Long Take*

i. April 29, 1992

This is not your city. What burns and whose likeness with the earth burns with it. When did you arrive only to leave again? Walking through wet cement. What does your longing mean. The sky asks who made a season as wretched as this. A man stands on his shop roof with a rifle pointed at the crowd. Another 'stood his ground and did his duty'. He 'got caught up in the frenzy'. You watched it on T.V., the suburbs greened and rolling. Over and over, a man, many men, they are all men, this much you think. 'Can we all just get along.' Wash and repeat, your mother says. Latasha Harlins, three years older than you, shot dead by somebody's Asian grandmother. A grandmother not unlike yours. She gets community service. Money in her hand. *Empire Liquor*, 91st and Figueroa, one of the first to go. The city is far away, the city is in your living room. A two-bedroom apartment in El Rio, California, once 'New Jerusalem'. America must have its monsters. It would take a long decade to change you from an American to an immigrant to a monster. Your likeness burns with it. The event is not itself but who is watching themselves being watched with relief. 'U just had a big time use of force', the cop types into his car dispatch, driving a victory lap round the precinct. *Officer officer overseer* (KRS-One). Chances are you have been looked upon with thoughts of violence. Not guilty. Devils. *Filthy* (Ice-Cube). *Today, the jury told the world that what we all saw with our own eyes was not a crime.* (Tom Bradley) *At the end of the small hours* (Aimé Césaire) *Everyone cried for himself | As the great noise descended | The beat of a thousand wings* (DS Marriott). For all that is yours. For all you have taken. Take this. This is not your city.

ii. April 17, 1993

You climb, arms over you, arms over your head. 188 feet into the air to drop and ply yourself from land again in loops of steel painted red. In the two and a half minutes this takes, two kinds of screams split the air from the ground. This is personal. Below, 'a mob' of black teenagers is angry about an oversold TLC concert. *Magic Mountain spokeswoman Eileen Harrell said park officials did nothing wrong. She blamed the violence on a crowd attracted by "that type of music".* Dropping 171 feet at an angle of 55 degrees, you go round again. Yesterday, a Federal court imprisoned Stacey Koon and Laurence Powell. This is not personal. You will have due process. You will have equal protection under the law. It was never personal. Running under a man's overcoat to the school bus, you lie down on the green vinyl seats and wait to be counted. Some of you are missing, others are crying. One is focused on a tennis ball-sized jaw breaker seized in his fist. A refugee from El Salvador whose first memory is a low flying plane you wrongly guessed was a crop duster. Luis believes he is a mutant, a saviour, a polymath, a Professor Xavier. He is waiting for his father who was disappeared. The park is emptying but he concentrates on it the white ball melting between his palms. Is personal. Helicopter searchlights flood the windows and rotate over your low breathing. Serpents of light and glass upend themselves in the dark, riding empty cars into the night.

iii. January 17, 1994

The old fault shakes our mountains, and rolls the San Fernando Valley's avenues into its song of buckled stucco and drywall. The smell of Vermont, Fairfax and Sepulveda burning. Folds of stone slither along a fissure that opens on your doorstep. A tremor, a riot, a verdict. Your step widens across the pavement. On the bank between sleep and death, you find your life at once to be so orderly. Unpatriated as you are by the parting of granite. Earth falls from an axe handed to your enemies in turns. Its dark soil burning. No reason then, to watch your well-built house, duly peopled, whiten to ash except that you might otherwise have refused to leave. Successive tremors fly. Dishes thick as cataracts wheel over the linoleum starboard hard and smash in the pitch. Something disturbing itself in the night has cracked the mock Tudor mould of your exile. An overpass crumbles out of view. Valley Fever beds into your lungs with the rising dust. It is Martin Luther King Jr. Day; it is Robert E Lee Day; it is almost 5 a.m. in the thin doorframe juddering between two rooms. That year, the neighbours wouldn't rebuild and left. What clings to you, you carry into another century. The cheapness of all you are obliged to call home. This is not personal. You recall without disgrace the borders you crossed, invisible but alive. Wrong question, you say, pointing your body to the west.

iv. April 11, 1994

This is not your history. There are two doors at the Museum of Tolerance: one, for those with prejudices and the other for those without, which is permanently locked. Inside, a whisper tunnel hurls prerecorded epithets at your classmates as they file through. Some giggle; some shout back. The thing you remember most clearly is eating a brownbag lunch as your eyes adjust. A white hot cement parking lot near Beverly Hills. This is personal. The film director Steven Spielberg is visiting Castlemont High School in Oakland at the request of state governor Pete Wilson, who is up for re-election. Earlier that year, on Martin Luther King Day, 69 mostly black Castlemont students were kicked out of a screening of *Schindler's List* for laughing at a concentration camp execution scene. A Nazi soldier casually shooting a Jewish woman. Psychiatrists were hauled in over the public uproar. The students wanted to watch *House Party 3*. Governor Wilson will be remembered for Proposition 187—a law denying illegal immigrants healthcare and education. At the assembly, Spielberg insists the kids received 'a very bad rap for what happened'. He'll come back, he promises, without the cameras. Most applaud the director of *E. T.* and *Jurassic Park*. Wilson has just signed the Three Strikes, habitual felon statute, into law. A campaign ad—grainy footage of people running across the Mexican border—warns, 'they're coming'. On the way home from the museum the school bus is rowdy. This is not personal. Your history teacher is visibly annoyed. Diane is not a natural blonde. She is a liberal feminist. She proudly poured coffee one summer for MLK in a southern diner, voted for every Kennedy. The LA freeways throw everything out of scale. 'I don't think I should have to take that history', Castlemont student Laronnda Hampton, 17, reportedly said. 'I don't even know my own history'.

v. October 3, 1995

This moving quarry on which you have landed carries on burning. Seneca, the only black student in the twelfth grade, bursts from the classroom, shouting—*my n***** is free, my n***** is free*—circling the school annexes where you sit in a row figuring the terminal velocity of a car travelling at speed against a wall without casualties. Your heroes are not good, your teachers proud; they pull the doors shut and let Seneca run himself tired. You gather your books and wait for it to be over. The physicist doubles as the girls' tennis coach. Holds court. He is a sentimental Europhile in a household of women. Every morning, he joins the prayer circle around the flag pole. They quote Pat Robertson into the onshore breeze. This is personal. The door is still shut. Outside, transplanted eucalyptus trees stand guard, dropping their tan sun-hardened skins. Parallax of shade and milk, axes x and y, the perfect state of *standard temperature and pressure* to whom all laws equally apply. Who is under siege. Who rattles the wall with their footsteps, fractures the cement. Who longs for the door to open, a leading out. Tracks that appear in the blood. Intersecting nowhere. A victory. A quarterback. Who stays on like this, until they die.

IV

On Desire.

(after Winckelmann)

What is *the gift?* To receive—she is touched,
or the scuttle of her heart is mollified by its touch.
O to be *touched* by the gift, like being singled out
and blessed by infirmity. The gift—
simulacrum of love—and he who gives it does so
knowing that by giving it to me nothing
could really be gained.

> Black corollary of love—
> *go trouble younger hearts.*

The man who wrote that phrase the breadth
of a single hair: *noble simplicity and grandeur*
also boasted: 'Ich esse gut und ich scheisse gut'.
He could articulate it, and wanting it, had that gift
of seeing that somewhere between these vivifications
of 'consummate' and 'evacuate'
is the completion of desire.

Eugenics of Art—
Homer mentions no pitted face, no pox. Arcangeli,
who would disembowel the Abbé, was not
the tone-deaf Olympian Alcibiades, fondling boys
in the gymnasium, but a disfigured man of no account.
Winckelmann wrote, much before his fated friendship:
The Archangel of Concha's *face*
'glows with indignation and revenge.'

*

Turning over rubble in the Villa Albani,
Winckelmann observes the broad repose of time.

Gleam of white light on a stone neck, on a pedestal of bone.
Perhaps some conquest, in a preternatural hour,
had carried off her head? Or trampled her face to dust.
Either way, he is sure that finding it is beyond his office.
The absence makes her animal.
He does not note this in his catalogue.

*

What had Rhodopis said, all those hours, to the ugliest of men?
When she heard his fables, what love stiffened
in the folds of garments that could hook itself
to the promise of one wayward slipper?

Chewing her thumbnail through his long-winded tale,
she may have at last excoriated:
'Enough of your riddles!'

Here is the apple and *there* is the tree, appearing ordinary.

*

Where is the tree? Despondent wife of Socrates
young and ancestrally equestrian.
Xantippe (meaning 'blonde horse') whom the old man
would not woo. He, a coquette in the world of men—
A gadfly—she could only buck.

*

True art in imitation
or true propaganda?

David's *Death of Socrates* alarmed the salon of 1787.

The scroll at Plato's feet. Death warrant… or versifications of Aesop?
Wise son of a midwife, who in his final hours
Reared like the horse of Napoleon Bonaparte.

        *

Slave of Samos, gnarled hunchback, deformed fabulist.
Your animal phrase soils the footstools of Europe.
There—and also there—a fleet of eyes, each identical
out-minister the other.

An unctuous industrialist pats his thorax.

Dissolute parthenogenist,
man vis-à-vis his instincts—
we sniff our own blood.

How you have multiplied in us
like an incandescence that hauls itself
up from the dark
to colour a woman's cheeks?

        *

Slave-girl, Cinder-girl, Horse-of-a-Different-Colour.
The wise busts of Herculaneum
angle the torsos of headless girls.

Withdrawing the candle from his window
that opens onto the Porta Salaria
Winckelmann carries thoughts of his pupil's contours
Down tapestried corridors to bed,
Following his moral windmill.

'Vivien With Household Gods'

[HB/PH/241-57: Photo Album of 57 Chester Terrace 1924–1929]

It is a matter between two wives, living and dead,
and who can guess where one ends and the other,
in shortened, enumerated breaths, begins
that loveless phrase of emptied rooms
and unpeopled letters:
yours in eternity.

One, colloidal with dust,
is powdering in upstairs rooms
by fireside lanterns of vinegar and gin,
desiccate widowhood mealing itself in air.
The other, besmattered and freaked with decay—
her face, razed by sunlight to purest whitewash,
turns towards her mantelpiece of household gods:
a silvery plate, pewter candlesticks and Hellenic vase—
its heroic scene a spear in the fist, muscular and poised to strike—
candles, a portrait of a lady in high-collars, jet beads, faraway in the eye.

V's hands are clasped
(as if she is trying not to touch them)
Her elbow rests lightly.

There can be only one priestess
at the altar of the fair husband.
Her prayerful look is excised
en toto, clean from the ears.

Tom & Polly & Peter (the dog and cat)
invigilate the changing of the shift.

V crumbles, inverts, wanders the streets in blackshirt
repeating the childhood question up to Stoke Newington
it's raining it's pouring and all the King's horses and all
in my lady's chamber and couldn't get up in the morning.

O O O all the King's men in Lancashire, in Hampstead,
in Compayne Gardens ringing me thin and ransacking
the house tedium deus protracted life ringing me thin
bring me gin by the fire on the lawn of Ottoline's garden.

[A Letter dated 14 September 1939 from TSE in London (on *Criterion* letterhead) to Richard Jennings: 'Your letter arrived timely to cheer me up: I have been plunged in dust, going through and destroying old papers which ought to have been destroyed years ago: turning up unanswered letters from people who are dead, a photograph of a man who has been in an insane asylum for years, and such cemetery matter.']

Nightmares at the Waldorf-Astoria

After Marilyn Monroe/Wallace Stevens

M enters, a golden imbricate
of mythic beauty. Stunning serpent
in the long grass of fluted columns.

She slept here. Semblance of the woman
one loves or ought to love.

Marble equipoise anxious
at the grand entrance.
Unaccustomed to the flop-house
or to God's long, long face.

On the ceiling, dead center,
tragic muse with a mask
of golden ringlets—

And yet, Marilyn is not a wild poem, fresh from Guatemala.
    Aqua Sancti—she dreams of excavation—
dark adventures into the whole of her creation.

> *to bring myself back to life*
> *has prepared me—given me*
> *whatever the hell it is.*

After the Fall—after a bottle and another bottle—
a woman sacrificed by her own hand or husband
to her pupils' black circumference.

> *and there is absolutely nothing there—*
> *there was absolutely nothing—*
> *finely cut sawdust—like out of a*
> *raggedy ann doll—the sawdust*

spills all over the floor & table
& hopes for theater are fallen.
Arthur is
disappointed—let down

(I stole four teaspoons from room 1614 and slept well)

there was absolutely nothing

Come to the Waldorf-Astoria!

Penitent arcade   of the Guerlain Spa
    where a man with enormous eyebrows
        dabs glycolic acid ecumenically
            Adieu, adieu mia cupola!

Once-brass bell-plates papered over in the 80s
    doors erupt onto dead porticos
        and valets emblazoned 'WA' approach
        gentlemen tendering ticket stubs,
        wrapped and civil in their livery.

Faces dipped in camphor: the Duchess Wallis, three Elizabeths,
(Windsors and Taylor), Princess Grace, lunatic and orchid-breasted.
All culpable Guineveres.
Does Mademoiselle—
who is very wealthy—
do borders?

In the wild country of the soul revolving
mirrors swing apart from fair forearms.
Despotic tableware fillets M's psyche, turtle-necked,
aqueous, framed in monochrome by books.

They serve swell board here.
Elsa Maxwell looks tired.   *O This terrible dis-ease.*

A sound in an adjoining room
an imagined body pacing lengths
of tired flesh.
                    For what, M wonders?

Woman has no natural home.
Return her floral tributes c/o.
At the edge of the mind someone's father—
        is that you, unlikely man of letters,
        dreaming of the tropics
        under an Imperial timepiece?—
        He waves a huge spray of greenbacks, agreeing.

A Good Wife

O Lord of the world, this is your lamplit service. You are the Arranger of the affairs of those humble beings who perform your devotional worship service. [Pause.] Lentils, flour and ghee—these things I beg of you. My mind shall ever be pleased. Shoes, fine clothes, and grain of seven kinds—I beg of you. A milk cow, and a water buffalo, I beg of you, and a fine Turkestani horse. A good wife to care for my home—your humble servant Dhanna begs for these things.
—Guru Granth Sahib

I am the snake in the box. You married me
after I strangled your horse. What service
was the wringing of its throat. This I beg
of you, your humble servant. The noise of
its two dry hind bones knocking together—
what a noise. The grain falling unripe from
its long stalk. Your continuous pleasure—
shoes, fine clothes, a buffalo—these things.

In the lamplight, any horse will do. But
you are particular, my Lord. Your home
is the shattering of glass bangles, drawing
blood. Colour. [Pause.] Lentils, flour, ghee.
I should have stripped the milk cow of
her soft, white buttocks. Who beguiles you,
heavy-eyed, with her sullen daily worship.

Something Particular

My aunt is in the kitchen. On the counter is a cup of tea. It is not precisely tea, but a boiled mix of leaves and spices with milk and sugar. Some would say this is another drink, an elsewhere. How my aunt makes it isn't a family secret but it is unique and no one not her mother not my mother not me makes it like she does, pinching and tearing as she swaps through the jars and into the water already simmering. Now it is green. And the house smells differently. She lifts the cup and pours it into the sink. It isn't cold. Her daughter falls out of the sky from an upstairs window onto a box, lately flattened for waste. She did not exactly drop in like an origami crane on a scatter of rough toys. In this way my aunt forgets her drink of no abstract use so quickly. A baize door slams like thunder. One corner of the picture this woman with her foreign drink. Another, the child swinging against an open window at play. Her husband, my uncle, is also my cousin but they are not really related by blood. The daughter is no primitive taboo whose shattered idol fears nothing in a back garden like this where no one saw her fall. Except her mother the tea already sweetening the metal socket of the drain. *I draw a black dot under your ear every morning to ward off evil and praise.* This means nothing or something particular to her.

Krampus

On the banks of Lake Fuschl the butter-coloured Schloss is ringed in snow. Emerald edged, glacial blue at its depth, a lakeside luxury hotel smothered by a valley of tall black pines. For a period of fifteen years in six hundred or so its fortress walls entertained officers making stiff one-armed salutes between courses of venison and sole at circular tables overlooking the wooded banks of the See. An old hunting lodge brushes up for the upright swine barking in their sunken pen of floor to ceiling windows as von Ribbentrop toasts the ear of the Führer over a bonfire of foreign gossip—Edward, he is sure, and Wallis stand firmly with the Reich. The dining room is almost level with the lake. You feel you could walk on it, the last unchanging vista on earth. The Schloss curates its losing. Its battlements are decorative; thick walls did little to deter the Anschluss and deportation of the house's previous owner—also a fascist. Von Ribbentrop, Hitler's man in Britain, is a champagne dealer by marriage, and the first Nazi to be hanged at Nuremberg. None of this features in rapturous descriptions of the hotel's fine aspect. You learn, only on returning home, facts that complicate the idyllic Salzburger charms of Christmas markets, Mozart marzipan chocolates that roll as both ball and bullet in your mouth. But didn't they point— you joked to your friends at home—like parody racists at you, your father, your mother, in the main square, in the restaurant, even the Schloss where you'd paid a migrant's ransom for the smallest room? And pointing, metamorphose into bearded devil-goats rampaging the streets, whipping tourists? Children at play; tradition for some, a ritual that sends you three fearful indoors. A vintage shop: iron plates, antique pistols, mishandled brooches and there, too, a porcelain bust of von Ribbentrop in military regalia, miraculous, honest as a slur.

Elsewhere

In Westwood, California, our professor,
whose name was, he told us proudly,
Yiddish for *fucker*, careened through Merrill.
Goethehaus I pronounced 'goathouse'
and the professor's modus
operandi was startled. Farnoosh scrawled
it wasn't me
on our copies of 'Lost in Translation'.
Who is Gunmoll Jean? We were too shy
to ask. But she did. Lee was all baseball.
Every verb was nude, and every girl extra innings.
It was 1999. Ty Warner was our D.W. Winnicott.
We stank of booze up and down Sunset Boulevard.

In Westwood, California
we were not Elizabeth Bishop, nor were we
her Aunt whose name is fiction.
As for Osa and Martin Johnson, *dressed in riding breeches*,
they were scheduling a sweet date while the *fucker*
yodelled on. *'Long Pig', the caption said.*
My dear F, it never occurred to us,
that yellow border around our necks.
Our modus operandi was shackled
to the knife in those *horrifying* breasts
we'd come to inherit without question.

I wish I'd known then about Osa and Martin.
The plane flying into the side of a mountain
queer as an animal appearing from the brush
regarding us like familiars. Death meant nothing
as we trampled through Lowell's *Life Studies*
never hearing the hesitation in his voice reciting

'For the Union Dead'—*that's what the despatches said*
—it might have meant something.
Flash. Bang.

In Newhall, Santa Clarita, the 'incident' that choked
in the throat of Stacey Koon in the decade
of our education no *pith helmets* could save
was not the crash but a blessing for violence.
How had I come to be here, / like them
and not know the century just beginning
would be our last. Together, this strangeness
would engender an earth's worth of unfamiliar
pictures, all unframed. The sound of telephone
lines going soft in a generation without
the children we birthed or didn't. Did we?
The family voice. Staring out into the Pacific alone.
But that moment *held us all together*
like the quiet before an exodus.
That *cry of pain* gathering in the margins
where one alights on what is worth taking—
carried through fire, my ancestors, a reliable syntax—
and what must be left behind.

Queens Astoria

Not one but two both useless. Women who have no use, evade use, betray use you women are these useless creatures. Useless where use is not determined, indeterminately useless women subpar all over the shop with your useless wittering on so useless is such uselessness. Flat in the face useless, over the edge, peculiarly useless from your palindrome of uselessness I read useless in many antiquated and extinct and exonerated defunct languages. Whatever uselessness you trade on the open market, however useless your synonymic imbricated functions of lack of use, the end of use the use that sees no other use but to drain heavily into the drain of uselessness that is you woman you are useless. I shout at your lack of present use, the hitching post of your uselessness the downtrodden borderline and bivalvic uselessness of your seafloor uselessness soundless as the ocean, the core principle of use. Back of the taxi useless, fine ermine useless what use is the figure of another woman dressed in the figure of my primarily female body that we inherit our uselessness from this kind of logic can have no use and makes for no useful conclusion. Concussive uselessness, uselessness that befits the stature of women in their unorthodox cheek sucking this is fine this is poor this is where I imitate a younger woman uselessness that evades the livery of useless clothing all women are in fact out of use if not out of fashion. We get swindled out of 10 dollars by a man of our own tribe. How useless are we not to scent our own after he told us we were without much use and then this man the prosecutor wants us to testify over the telephone against our taxi driver *well now there's a story*

Acknowledgements

Thanks, as ever, are due to Tony Frazer at Shearsman for letting me get on with things without much interference.

I am grateful to the editors of magazines and anthologies that published these poems before they found this book shape: Ilya Kaminsky for *Ploughshares*, Emily Berry at *The Poetry Review*, guest editors Richard Scott and Andre Bagoo at *The Poetry Review*, Alex Houen and Adam Piette at *Blackbox Manifold*, Gboyega Odubanjo and Joe Carrick-Varty at *bath magg*, Jeet Thayil for *The Penguin Book of Indian Poets*. And to Helen Tyson for inviting me to the University of Sussex to speak about *Faust* and (sort of) modernism.

Thanks also to those who generously offered feedback on these poems along the way: Valzhyna Mort, Bhanu Kapil, Sarah Howe, Ilya Kaminsky, Anthony Anaxagorou, Fred D'Aguiar, Fiona Curran, Sara Crangle, Dinah Roe, Nuar Alsadir, Deryn Rees-Jones, Rachael Allen, Sam Solnick, David Hering, Anne Enderwitz, Vidyan Ravinthiran, Forrest Gander. To James and our beloved Gaia. And to my parents and my sister, Parveen, for many lifetimes of striving.

Finally, thanks are owed for permission to quote lines from Dorothea Lasky's poem, 'The Miscarriage', from the volume *Milk* (2018), to the author and to Wave Books; likewise, thanks are owed to BOA Editions for permission to quote an excerpt from Lucille Clifton's 'the lost baby poem', from *How to Carry Water: Selected Poems*. Copyright © 1987, by Lucille Clifton. Reprinted with the permission of The Permissions Company, LLC on behalf of BOA Editions, Ltd., boaeditions.org.

Lightning Source UK Ltd.
Milton Keynes UK
UKHW010717130722
405782UK00001B/39